NAUGHTY NANA

Written by
SARALYN RICHARD

Illustrated by
REBECCA EVANS

NAUGHTY NANA
©2013 Saralyn Richard
All rights reserved. No part of this publication may be reproduced, stored in a retrieval system, or transmitted, in any form or by any means, electronic, photocopying, recording, or otherwise, without the prior written permission of the publisher.

Published by Palm Circle Press, LLC.

Printed in the United States of America
First Edition

ISBN: 978-0-9896255-0-0
ISBN: 978-0-9896255-1-7
Library of Congress: 2013914305

To purchase this book, visit: www.palmcirclepress.com or www.saralynrichard.com.
Join the Naughty Nana Fan Club at www.palmcirclepress.com/naughtynana.

Printed in the United States by Bookmasters, Inc.
30 Amberwood Parkway, Ashland, OH 44805
Aug. 2013

Job# M11198

This book is dedicated to the dogs in our family,
and to the children who love them unconditionally.

Naughty? Me? I'm just a sheepdog puppy who wants to have fun. I am the one with the white flower on my bottom. It wiggles when I shake my rear end.

One day while I am happily digging in mud, I am dragged in for a bath and brushing. Some people must be coming to look at us puppies and take one home. I'm going to wiggle my flower, so they will like me best!

Ding dong! In come two grownups, Grammy and Papa, and another dog, too. His name is Bogey. He is a Scotty with perfect manners.

I wiggle my flower to get Bogey to have some fun. He sniffs, looks me up and down, and walks away. But I am being good! Will Grammy and Papa pick me to join their family?

They pick me! Grammy leads me to the car, where we sit, while Papa drives for many miles and hours. I am afraid to leave my doggy family, and I am a little afraid of Bogey, too, so I just curl up and sleep all the way home.

Finally, we arrive at my new house. Everyone is very tired, but not me. I zip around and bark!

Grammy builds a bed for me in the kitchen, with a pillow and newspapers. I don't like it one bit! So I bark, "No! No!" Grammy tries reading Bogey and me to sleep. I just chew on the book!

The next morning, Papa shows me the back yard. I show him how I love to dig. I make six deep holes in Grammy's garden faster than Papa can stop me.

"No, no, Nana! Naughty Nana," Papa cries, chasing me around the yard. I smile with glee. *I am going to like this yard!*

Later, I speed around the house, looking for fun. I find it in the bathroom, where I undo the entire roll of toilet paper, building a soft, squiggly pile. When Grammy sees my paper mountain, she cries, "No, no, Nana! Naughty Nana!" I wonder why Grammy is so upset.

"Have you seen my keys?" Papa asks, as Grammy cleans up the mess. Papa and Grammy look everywhere, but can't find Papa's keys.

Jason and Gaby, Grammy's and Papa's grandchildren, are coming soon, so we go out to practice playing with children in the neighborhood. Luckily, there is a children's birthday party at the end of the block. Girls and boys are jumping in a bounce house.

I wiggle my flower as I pull Papa toward the fun. Some children run out to pet me, oohing and aahing at how cute I am. Papa holds my leash tightly so I won't jump on anyone. *Don't worry, kids, I'm fun to play with!*

Just as Papa starts to relax, I run toward the bounce house. It looks delicious! Before anyone can stop me… I take a big bite out of the castle. "No, no, Nana! That is naughty!" *It might be naughty,* I think, *but it is fun!*

Finally Jason and Gaby come to visit Grammy and Papa. I am so excited that I zip around them in circles. This sends Jason screaming, "Noooooo, Nana!" *Why doesn't Jason want to play with me?*

Gaby tries to make me stop being naughty. Papa holds Gaby close, and tells her, "You are the boss of Nana. You just tell her in a strong voice what you want her to do."

From then on, Gaby says to me, "Nana, no biting, only kisses!" or "No jumping, only hugs!" And, because Gaby is so patient and sweet, I listen *most* of the time.

Meanwhile, Jason calls to Grammy, "Have you seen my hairbrush?"

"No, but things seem to be disappearing around here."

Everyone looks for the missing hairbrush and Papa's keys, but neither can be found. Gaby stares at me, but I look away.

That afternoon we go to the beach. I am going to *try* to be good! I am so excited that I tug hard at my leash. Even strong Papa has a hard time controlling me. Suddenly I squeal, and Papa shouts, "Oh, no!"

I have fallen from the seawall! *Ouch!* I land far below. Papa hands the leash to Grammy and runs two blocks to the stairs, so he can reach me. I try to climb up the curved wall, but I keep slipping down. "No, no, Nana. Stay where you are. Papa is coming to get you," Gaby calls.

I never want to pull away from Papa again!

After Papa rescues me, I am ready to play on the beach. Gaby and Jason walk with me at the edge of the water. When a wave laps at our feet, everyone splashes and kicks, but I bark at the wave, as if to say, *"No, no, Wave. Naughty wave!"*

Jason picks up a stick and writes, "Jason loves Nana." Then I grab the stick in my teeth and run away with it. *Is that naughty?*

Then, I find a place where tiny clams are wiggling in the wet sand. I use my paws to dig a bigger hole. How I love to dig! I tilt my head as if to say, *"No, no, Clams! Naughty Clams!"* When Gaby catches up to me, I look up with a ring of mud on my face and give her lots of sandy kisses.

A muddy face means another bath and brushing, but I don't mind with Jason and Gaby around. When I hop out of the tub, Papa enters the room, saying, "I can't find my pen.

Grammy says, frowning, "We've never had so many lost things. Nana, do you know where they are?"

I just wiggle my flower at Grammy and go to play with Gaby, who never calls me naughty. But I don't like the way I feel inside.

I roll over and let Gaby's fingers tickle my tummy…It is the quietest I have ever, ever been. *I feel happy when Gaby calls me nice.*

After dinner, I nudge Gaby. "Nice Nana," says Gaby. "Do you want to go outside?" I zip toward the door. "I want to take her outside," Gaby says, "all by myself." So everyone stands by the doorway, watching quietly, while Gaby and I go outside together.

"Nice Nana!" Gaby says. I run to Gaby, giving her sloppy kisses. Then I run to the pretty flowers, making a scrunching turn and zipping back to Gaby. I decide then to show Gaby my special secret.

"What are you doing, Nana?" Gaby asks. She bends to look under one of the flower bushes, where something is sticking up from the dirt.

"Oh, Nana! Is this Papa's pen?" I look up at Gaby and smile. Everyone runs to the spot. Sure enough, there is the tip of Papa's pen. Jason grabs a stick and starts digging, and guess what he finds?

Not just a pen, but also a hairbrush and the keys to the house! I have led Gaby to my special hiding place! Everyone gives me lots of hugs and praise, happy to have solved the mystery, and happy that I am not naughty anymore. Bogey just looks at me and nods.

And you know what? I *like* being Nice Nana!